Comforts of Home

Comforts of Home

TAILOR-MADE, FAMILY-FRIENDLY INTERIORS THAT FEEL JUST RIGHT

Andrew Howard

Written with Andrew Sessa

ABRAMS, NEW YORK

Contents

Introduction

Oh, hi. Hey. Welcome back. Thanks for cracking open *Comforts of Home*. Glad to have you here for Book Two—or, as I like to call it, *Andrew Howard: Return of the Redecorator*. (Good, right? No? OK, we'll workshop it and get back to you.)

It's been a few years since I first had the chance to invite you into the pages of a book filled with photos of homes I've created for all sorts of families, some of them probably a lot like yours. Since then, I've been running around, working on a whole bunch of houses across the country. Some have been for families I've had the pleasure of helping before, others have been for people new to me, but all of them have overflowed with different possibilities and different ideas of what "home" can be and what it can mean.

As for me and my family, my boys—who were just seven and ten when I started working on my first book, *Style Comfort Home*, in the spring of 2020—are now thirteen and sixteen, with all the big feelings and bigger sports padding that come with it. Along with my amazing wife, Katie, we moved into a new house in Jacksonville, Florida, that we designed and built from the ground up. We lived in it for six months with virtually no furniture and then another six months with not a whole lot more than a sofa and four barstools. Let's call it a learning experience and leave it at that. I'm not sure I've ever appreciated a real bed—let alone a fully decorated house—quite as much as I did when we finally finished ours.

The experience of designing and creating this new home gave me a new appreciation for how lucky I am to help other people create theirs. And it taught me a lot more about what it takes to make a house a home, especially a home that's as personal and family-friendly as we wanted ours to be, and I know all of you want yours to be, too. That's a big part of what led me to write this book for you. I wanted to share all I've learned about what good, thoughtful, tailor-made, *fun* design can do for you and your loved ones.

Now felt like the right time to show you what I've been up to lately. I hope that by losing yourself in this book's pages, you can also find yourself—in a family whose story sounds like yours or in a house that looks and feels the way you want yours to.

In my first book, I used pictures of many houses I'd designed, all broken up into different parts and in different ways to help readers find their style: There was a section on kitchens here, another on decorating with tons of patterns there. That let the book serve kind of like a how-to guide, and also sort of like an à la carte menu—one that encouraged you to try and taste ideas and strategies piece by piece.

With this book, I wanted to show you how an entire room—and an entire house—come together, to let you see how a home's design can flow from one space to the next. That'll help you understand how to turn any space and every home into so much more than the piece-by-piece sum of its parts.

The first step in getting there relies on coming up with the inspiration and vision for your whole house. The best way to figure that out? Looking at tons of photos of other houses. And conveniently, in your hands right now, you've got a whole book filled with photos of other houses. Congratulations! You've found a great place to start.

Checking out images of other people's homes is how you learn what you want for yours—and, just as important, what you *don't* want. Then, everything else about your design can flow from there, which makes things easy. You pick pieces that match your overall vision.

To make it even simpler, in this book, I've broken things down into three styles that most of my projects fit into: formal but still fun, relaxed but still put together, neutral but still exciting. I guarantee you, one of these looks will work for you and your family. Scout's honor.

It's not just about what a room looks like that lets it feel like home and work for you, however. Turning your dreams into a dream house means ensuring your interiors meet your family's more logistical needs. Do you want rooms that are lovely to look at? Yes, sure, of course. And you deserve them, too. But there are so many more considerations that anyone with a kid (or two) or a dog (or three) or a spouse (or . . . hey, you do you!) knows they've got to think about.

I always ask the families I work with

to tell me about how they live, from the everyday (What is your morning routine like? How about the evening?) to the special occasion (How many people, absolute max, does the house need to host for holidays? What's your tolerance for indoor football after Thanksgiving dinner?).

This is important because we don't just *look* at our houses, we actually *live* in them, too. And because none of us have enough time for all the stuff we're trying to do in a day, or enough room for all the things we're trying to cram into our basement or attic, my goal is always to design a home that can help everything be simpler. I want it to be easier to do all the things and to store all the stuff.

Throughout this book, you'll find little boxes on what I'm calling "Life Lessons"—design ideas and advice that can help your house work better for you. A lot of these come from things I learned when designing my own home, from the thrill of working with an artist friend to create our own custom wallpaper to the relief I experienced when I remembered I upholstered a sofa with washable indoor-outdoor fabric right after Katie spilled an entire bowl of chili on it.

These days, we are spending more time at home than ever before. And that's a good thing. It means home, and family, matter more than ever before. At the same time, life is probably full of a lot more headaches than it used to be. That's not a good thing. But being able to savor the good times and, yeah, even deal with the bad ones in a home that feels like it's your very own special space? That makes the good times even better and the bad ones at least a bit easier.

Home is special. It's the only place in the world where you have full control. So you get to design it just the way you want it to be. A million years ago—OK, just sixty, but who's counting?—in the TV special *Rudolph the Red-Nosed Reindeer*, Burl Ives said something like, "The world looked a lot more complicated than it seemed when you were snug and warm at home." That snug and warm feeling is what lets you forget about all your problems, all those complications, and lets your home become your happy place.

I'm all about finding that happy place, and I made this book to help you find yours. Let's get going.

RELAXED

BUT STILL PUT TOGETHER

Relaxed interior design sometimes gets a bad rap. I think that's because it suggests a certain messiness, like all loose slipcovers, overstuffed armchairs, and wrinkly linen curtains. Or because it makes people think your kids decorated your house when they were at their most feral (which, in the case of my boys, is every school night from dinner till bedtime and every weekend morning at 7 A.M., if not 5 A.M.). But none of that needs to be true. I'm here to rehabilitate the reputation of "relaxed."

First off, it doesn't need to look sloppy. When you're relaxed, does that mean you've got to be in pajamas with bedhead and some breakfast cereal on your chin? No, no it does not. Relaxed means at ease, at peace, and, importantly, comfortable being yourself. It's more self-care than letting yourself go.

Basically, it's a decorating style you can feel extremely comfortable relaxing in. We all deal with a lot—and I mean a lot—during our day to day. Nothing seems easy, and stress is part of life. That's OK (or almost OK) when you're at the office, but when you get home, you just want to let it all go. I'd like to think that the way my spaces encourage relaxation is one of the main reasons people call me to help them design their homes.

But what does this look actually look like? For me, it sits in that so-called "transitional" space between truly traditional (often too formal to be really relaxed) and purely contemporary (often too sleek to be truly comfortable).

You'll see more small prints than large ones, and more solids overall; more color than monochrome; more wicker, bamboo, and painted or light woods than dark finishes; more granite than marble; and plenty of upholstery and pillows. At the same time, there's less embellishment and fewer layers of pattern and texture. You'll also notice less stuff out than in a more formal home. Not that a formal look is cluttered, exactly, but it often comes with more collections of art, antiques, and other objects.

As a result of all this, relaxed spaces can serve more of a rough-and-tumble lifestyle, even if they don't look it. These homes are less fragile, less breakable, than more formal residences. But they don't have to be any less stylish.

This look can often be perfect for families with younger kids—especially people who are starting to design a home without already having a ton of vintage pieces, heirlooms, or art. It's also great for empty nesters who expect they'll be hosting kids and grandkids.

To me, relaxed design is all about large gatherings, great meals served family style, and easy-flowing conversation. It creates a home that people love to visit again and again and again. These houses have rooms that are perfect for watching a game in, with popcorn crumbs everywhere, but also have some more adult spaces where parents can hang out for grown-up chatter, away from tiny ears and sticky hands.

The relaxed look can work especially well in a house with fewer architectural details and a bit less built-in character inside and out, and it's a good fit as well in a smaller house, where you don't have the space for a formal living room, a semi-sophisticated den, and a separate play space for the kids.

In this section, we'll take a look at four houses whose owners all, for one reason or another, thought relaxed was right for them. Sometimes the family's lifestyle dictated this look; other times it was the owners' personal style, the style of the architecture of their house, or the specifics of its setting.

Whatever the reason, each home makes its owners just say "ahhhhh"—like they're at a spa, not like they're at the dentist or the ENT—as soon as they walk in the front door.

At Home with the Howards

THE JACKSONVILLE HOUSE WE DESIGNED FOR OURSELVES MAY VERY WELL SURPRISE YOU

I don't think I'd ever fully appreciated living in a completely furnished—and finished—house until my family and I spent close to a year in our not-quite-completed new place in Jacksonville with not much more than a sectional sofa, four barstools, and a few mattresses on the floor. This hadn't been our original plan at all, no way, no how. At the last minute, the family that bought our former home decided they wanted all our furniture, too. Not a bad compliment, right? The problem was, it left us starting from square one when it came to filling the new house.

You'd think I'd be able to get furnishings fast, but when you're an interior designer, meeting clients' needs always comes first—I swear!—and that, plus some very, very, very long supply chain delays, meant Katie, the boys, and I were essentially camping out in our home for twelve very, very, very long months.

I commissioned this mural to recall our great memories of a family trip to Nantucket. Can you spot our boys in it? (One thinks his rear end looks too big, but otherwise, there were no ifs, ands, or, uh, buts about hanging this here.) **PREVIOUS PAGES AND PAGE 13:** The vibrant botanical fabric used for the living room's walls and curtains inspired my palette for much of our house. It grabs your attention the moment you step inside and see it from the foyer.

But you know what? I wouldn't trade that time for anything (though I'm also pretty sure I wouldn't do it again, or recommend anyone else try it). First off, it was, weirdly, kind of fun, and second, it taught us so much about how we would use the house, which we built from scratch with residential designer Kevin Gray. We learned what rooms we gravitated toward more than others, which spaces got the best light at certain times of day. And all that helped me make a whole bunch of design decisions. Take my office as an example, or the room I *thought* I'd claim as my office. During those long no-furniture days, I realized I wasn't going to need a space that big to work from—especially since I liked going into my actual office—and that its coziness, relatively small windows, and closeness to the bedrooms would make it a great media room.

Our previous homes had also taught us a lot about what we needed in this new one, especially in terms of space planning—all things I think any young family can benefit from. We knew we wanted a larger kitchen (duh) and dining areas, too, plus an extra chill-out room for the kids. We also hoped to have an adults-only area other than our bedroom and the living room—one that was a bit removed from the rest of the house. Lastly, we wanted an uber-comfortable group lounging zone, in addition to the family room, for watching TV—which is the media room that my office became.

ABOVE AND OPPOSITE: I wanted to have botanical prints up and down the walls of our staircase. But my sons' never-quite-clean, never-quite-kept-to-themselves hands meant the pictures would never stay neat and tidy. Instead, I designed millwork to look like picture frames, and then had artist Bob Christian paint the images inside them.

I lacquered the ceiling of our kitchen to help reflect natural light from the adjacent family room; that's a trick I've returned to again and again when designing rooms that don't have their own windows. The repeated lattice pattern used on the cabinet doors, island base, and backsplash could have been too much, but because it appears in slightly different ways in each spot, it turned out to be just enough.

A lot of these must-have spaces are now my favorite rooms in the house. But before we get to them, I'm sure you're wondering about the big picture of how we wanted our home to look and feel. So here goes.

Mostly, we were led by how we wanted it to feel because, believe it or not, I didn't know exactly how I wanted it to look. (Is that a dangerous thing for an interior designer to admit about his own house? If so, stop reading right now, and just go look at all the pretty pictures.)

I designed the house one room at a time, without an overarching aesthetic vision other than wanting it all to be colorful and memorable. For the most part, I started each space with what I thought was a cool idea or lead fabric—many I'd originally had for clients but hadn't used because they weren't a fit. I'd saved all my favorites, and I broke out a ton of them to use here. A breakfast nook wrapped in an oversize gingham check? Check. A wildly colorful botanical print for both the walls and the curtains in the living room? Double check. Custom mural wallpapers in five different rooms? Quintuple check.

As for that former office turned media room, it takes inspiration from Elvis's famous plant-covered Jungle Room at Graceland. I'll admit that particular inspo wasn't something I'd ever pitched to a client, but the kids heard about the King's space and thought it would be great to have something similar somewhere

ABOVE: Our dining area is the breakfast nook I always dreamed of having when I was growing up, and it has a little bit of a retro-diner look as a result. A stained hardwood table, vinyl-upholstered diner-style banquette, and faux-leather chair cushions make it all but indestructible, but no less stylish. **OPPOSITE:** Butler's pantries aren't just for butlers and scullery maids anymore! Bartenders love 'em, too. Ours becomes the drinks station during every party we have.

in the house. I didn't want our family home to be filled only with my (great, super-awesome) ideas, and the little people had spoken. Now, we have a palm-print-wrapped Jungle Room, and we all love it. Twelve people can fit on the sectional in there, easy.

OK, but back to how we wanted the house to feel: The main thing was just totally relaxed. As I've said before, to me, the number one way to make a house like this comfortable is to be sure it's indestructible. And this one absolutely is: all indoor-outdoor fabrics and carpets, washable painted surfaces, flooring and wall coverings made of vinyl that look like wood or paper. When the adults in a house aren't worried about things getting destroyed, everyone gets to be entirely, completely, at ease.

Whatever the style, I think the biggest sign of a home's success is when people want to come over. Like, when I drive by a house I've designed for folks and I see a pile of bikes and a bunch of cars in the driveway, I know I've done my job right. And, yeah, I know a lot of that is about the people who live there. But it's also about how a house makes the people in it feel: comfortable, and maybe even like their truest and best selves. When that's the case, people just want to be there, and that's definitely what has happened with our place. Our kids' friends suggest we host the next sleepover, and neighbors stop by unannounced, somehow ending up in our kitchen. I guess it could just be my cooking, or my what's-not-to-love personality? Nah, it's definitely the house.

Inspiration is everywhere. I noticed this striped wallpaper in a scene in *Home Alone* and asked my wallpaper maker to re-create it for our family room. As for the sofa on the right, that's the one my wife, Katie, spilled an entire bowl of chili on the week we got it. Because I'd had the foresight to cover it in outdoor fabric, our marriage is still intact. Oh, and there's no stain on it, either.

ABOVE AND OPPOSITE: Main suites can often be too masculine or too feminine, but ours strikes a good balance by being mostly neutral, with a floral wall covering in the bedroom and then blue in the bath. Katie and I both wanted our space to feel a bit quieter than the rest of the house, which I'd otherwise filled with big and bold decorating ideas.

Always give yourself the chance to go a bit over the top with your decorating in a guest bedroom. That way, guests who find your style to be too much—and what sort of friends are they, anyway?—won't overstay their welcome. I pulled the motif on the walls here from something Katie and I saw on a favorite trip to Italy.

CHELSEA FC

LIFE LESSON

A Place for Memories

As much as a house is a place for making new memories, it can also be for celebrating ones you've already made. That's a huge part of how you can add personality to a design and help a house become a home. When it came to designing our house, I knew I wanted to incorporate a bunch of different family favorites: The art in the media room, for instance, is of New York, the kids' go-to city to visit. The adults-only bar off the living room is painted green in homage to the color of my favorite college pub. Having a drink there now, I feel like my old self (as opposed to just feeling like myself, but old). Our younger son's room has a fine art piece based on *Field of Dreams*, a beloved movie of his, while our older son's, seen here, has a painting we commissioned of a few pairs of his favorite sneakers. The guest bedroom incorporates a bunch of motifs Katie and I saw and fell in love with on a trip to Florence for an Italian wedding. And the dining room plays with fun stuff we saw on a family summer holiday in Nantucket. Having dinner there brings back great memories from one of our best vacations of all time.

Yeah, I've indoctrinated my kids into the pattern-on-pattern-on-pattern look. Neither of our boys has complained yet. But there's still time! I'll let you know if they're demanding minimalist all-white or all-black spaces in their rebellious late-teenage years. The look works here because of the familiar red, white, and blue color scheme and the fact that many of the prints subtly echo each other, just at different scales and in varied motifs.

ABOVE: My boys convinced me to turn our media room into an homage to the Jungle Room at Graceland, and I'm glad they did. But I had to draw the line at a shag-carpeted ceiling, even if that's what Elvis had. **OPPOSITE:** This is our no-kids-allowed room. Every house should have one. There's a screen opposite the sofa, and since this room is away from the rest of the house, we don't wake the kids if a movie or football game gets loud. **PREVIOUS PAGES:** I might have made this bunk room a little too playful. Our kids often prefer spending the night here than in their own rooms. And who can blame them?

KNOB
CREEK

Bahamas Barefoot Chic

A FEET-IN-THE-SAND CARIBBEAN RETREAT DESIGNED FOR A COUPLE WITH DREAMS OF GRANDKIDS

I don't want to complain, but sometimes my job is pretty tough. Not like Superman-stopping-Lex-Luthor-to-save-the-world tough, but, still, it can be hard. I mean, a guy could almost drown in fabric samples, to say nothing of the back-breaking labor of having to tell someone where to put a twelve-ton piece of countertop marble. Whew. You can't help but sweat, you know?

There was nothing tough about this project, however. When a family asks you to create a resort-like getaway for their extended family on a pristine five acres of water-view property on a tiny island in the Bahamas, there's almost no way to go wrong. Who couldn't relax with that ocean and sky, and those Caribbean breezes?

STYLE COMFORT HOME
ANDREW HOWARD
Mrs. Howard Room by Room

Still, this house wasn't entirely without its challenges. Chief among them was making sure the interiors didn't distract from, or compete with, the amazing natural surroundings. Instead, the rooms needed to complement them. And then there was this: Even though the homeowners were extremely adventurous when it came to pattern and color, they didn't want any of it on the walls or ceilings. None. Anywhere. Just straight-up white. No paint in another hue. Certainly no wallpaper. What's a designer to do?

I'll tell you what a designer (well, this designer, anyway) does—and why it worked. The all-white-painted wooden walls ended up giving the place a crisp, carefree, classically Caribbean look that immediately suggested the relaxed atmosphere the homeowners wanted. Those walls are also easy to care for, and that means this house is easy and anxiety-free to live in, especially important when you've got dreams of little grandchildren running around. All you have to do is paint over scratches or chips when they happen. (And they will happen, trust me.)

From there, the family's comfort with bright colors and bold patterns—for use anywhere other than on the walls—turned into a major advantage. It ensured there'd be no lack of fun anywhere, even as the white walls let things remain cool and just calm enough.

To keep the views top of mind, we complemented the surroundings by pulling colors directly from the outside: the blues and greens of the house's surroundings during daylight hours and the yellows, pinks, and oranges of sunrise and sunset. Consider the living room—its soothing aqua and soft verdant shades are exactly what you see when you look out the windows: lush landscaping with ocean, sky, and sea beyond.

It also helped the scheme here that the homeowners have great taste. On one of our first meetings, we went to a design center, and they pulled some fantastic, big, bold colorful textiles that we ended up using as curtains in two of the bedrooms, where the print gave us the palette for the whole space. (When picking fabrics, they went even bigger and bolder than I might have otherwise, and it was great.)

This place has six bedrooms. But none of them are guest bedrooms exactly. That's because each was specifically designed for one of the homeowners' sons or daughters. And a big part of this house's success—both in terms of how it looks and how it works for the family—comes from the fact that each of the kids had some say in the design of their space. The parents and I worked out the big

OPPOSITE, PREVIOUS PAGES, AND PAGE 37: I wouldn't say formal dining rooms are dead. But it's becoming common to see a dining table hang out between the kitchen and the seating area in what is basically one big living room. Doing that at this Bahamas home invites a crowd and a party, which is exactly what the homeowners wanted. Check out the mix of slightly rustic, oh-so-casual materials, soft indoor-outdoor fabrics, and prints of different scales.

DEAN CORNWELL
FROM LANDS OF TROPIC SPLENDOR BANANAS COME TO YOU
FULL OF NATURE'S GOODNESS, WITH MATCHLESS FLAVOR TOO
beach roaming
GQ

Even in a relaxed house, some spaces will be a bit more formal and some a bit more casual. This family room is for sure in that second camp. We punched up the saturation a ton from the living-dining area and added a broader variety of colors into the mix, even though we stuck mostly with blue and green. Patterns are bolder and bigger, too. And how about that wild pillow mix? The sectional is especially people- and dog-friendly, and is a favorite spot in the house to kick back.

ideas, but the next generation got to weigh in big-time, too. That helps the house feel relaxed, because the best family houses are ones where we listen to what each member of the family wants.

Something everyone in this family wanted was plenty of space to gather all together, both indoors and out, and we gave them that. This house can comfortably sleep ten adults plus another two to four little kids easy, and it's got all the sofas, loungers, table space, and dining chairs they'd need. There's nothing worse in a house like this than having a big group over and finding you all need to decamp to different rooms to find a place to sit down or eat. That's why the dining room easily seats a dozen, and the living room does, too.

Here's one final thing about a home that encourages relaxation. It's got to be worry-free, and this one certainly is. Even in its most put-together spaces, you've got sisal rugs that wear well, outdoor fabrics on the sofas, and floors that won't show sand or dust, plus surfaces that are universally approved for putting down drinks with no coasters.

Sometimes we say a house is worry-free, and it's really not. But this one absolutely is. I'd have no problem turning three or four toddlers and three or four dogs loose in here all at the same time. Just don't ask me to put them to bed afterward, especially if it involves a book with a lot of words and very few pictures.

LIFE LESSON

Easy-care Style

In a vacation house that's meant to be carefree, the last thing you want is to walk in from the beach or pool and have to ask, "But where can I sit?" All your furniture has got to be able to withstand dripping-wet bathing suits and towels, sandy feet, and spilled dark 'n' stormies. And it can all be attractive, too. This house made that possible with wood walls painted crisp white (which makes cleaning and touch-ups a breeze) and floors of wide-planked oak (some of the most beautiful and hardest wood out there) with a light stain that helps sand all but disappear. Color here comes from the fabrics and furnishings, nearly all of which were designed for outdoor use but absolutely have the sophisticated look and soft hand feel of indoor versions. There is honestly nothing that could be done to destroy this house. And believe me, I know what a five-year-old's birthday party can do to a sofa and a rug. People talk about wanting to relax and put their feet up anywhere, and here you actually can.

The owners of this house wanted all-white wooden walls everywhere, which is a very beachy-Caribbean look. Great. But they also told me they wanted lots of color and pattern. I took that challenge head-on and made big statements with window treatments and almost every stitch of upholstery, plus painted furniture, tile, artwork, and much more. The white walls help the colors pop. **PREVIOUS PAGES:** As the bedrooms in this house go, the owners' has the most serene style. It's somewhat pared back compared to the others, so it feels like an especially soothing sanctuary.

Casual Island Living

A GROWN-UP PLAYHOUSE FOR EMPTY NESTERS WITH IMAGINATION TO SPARE

When the owner of this house first got in touch with me, I told her—multiple times—that I thought she was prank calling me. For weeks before, I'd been talking to everyone in my studio about how all I wanted was to do a granny-chic project, with lots of bold, bright patterns and color, plus chinoiserie and other classic styles that we could rework in new, unfussy ways. I'd become so obsessed, I'd even put together a mood board.

So when I got the call . . . I thought it had to be a prank from one of the junior designers on staff. But it wasn't.

The client and her husband had a subdued late-twentieth-century home on Georgia's Saint Simons Island, and they thought I could help take it from understated to statement making. To get the job done, they wanted it all: all the patterns, all the prints, all the colors, with every room getting a different palette than the one before. There was never enough color for these two—like, truly, never enough.

Sometimes this hunger for having all the things is a good thing, and sometimes it's a bad thing, but in this case, it was a great thing. The house they'd bought—for themselves, but also for visits from their grown kids and grandchildren—wasn't very large or architecturally interesting. And that's the perfect type of house to go (just shy of) overboard on. Mixing in lots of different prints and hues helps distract the eye from the lack of interior details.

Beyond color and pattern, this couple loved vintage pieces and antiques, too. They had accumulated a ton of furniture over the years, and when I went to look at it, I felt like I was thrifting at one of the best shops in Palm Beach. This was especially exciting because the couple wanted every room to tell a story, and there's no better way to do that than with

Thanks to the fun green leopard print on the traditional chairs and the crazily colorful botanicals I asked Bob Christian to paint on the paneled wall, this coastal Georgia home's sitting room seamlessly combines the relaxed and the formal. **PREVIOUS PAGES:** A good all-season porch lets you imagine you're playing outside even if the weather isn't playing along. Vintage wicker and a blue-and-green palette help this one do that with ease.

COASTAL BLUES Phoebe Howard
THE JESUITS and the ARTS

one-of-a-kind pieces. And the ones with the best stories to tell? You guessed it: antiques.

The owners' vintage items all had a casual, comfortable look—they weren't nose-in-the-air, capital "A" antiques, which was perfect, because the couple hoped their home could be casual, comfortable, collected, and worn in in the best possible way. And that's just the way many of the best vintage items are too, if you think about it.

While some of these spaces—the living room especially—may seem formal at first, once you walk around or have a seat, you realize it's all layered, collected, and cozy. You'll find soft, sink-in-able cushions and almost no tight tailoring. And because the furnishings are old but not extremely precious, it's OK to put your feet up on anything. Layers of color and pattern show you just how casual it all is, and the consistent fairly traditional style keeps it from becoming a hodgepodge.

The sun porch is a prime example. We tented the ceiling with a green-and-white small-scale floral fabric, using it again on a set of dining chairs, then doubled and tripled down on the color scheme (and the pattern mix) with a geometric trellis-motif rug and a corner banquette covered with a topiary garden pattern and fringed on the bottom edge. Relaxed wicker, cane, rattan, and bamboo antiques, all newly painted white, balance any stiffness or stuffiness, and the whole thing plays off the high-contrast view outside. There you've got pink-and-white cabana-stripe chaise lounges and sun umbrellas with gathered skirting.

For the homeowners' bedroom, we went with a red-and-white checked dust ruffle and curtains, aqua-hued ginger jar lamps, antique rattan bedside chests, and a vintage bed—all in a space we had clad in a pagoda-dotted chinoiserie wallpaper with a fern green ceiling. We really leaned into the mandate that more is more, but we kept it all casual, too.

The clients gave us the framework for what they wanted and then let us go pretty wild here. And I think that is a big part of what makes the house so successful: We made sure it flows perfectly from room to room, even as each room tells its own story, as does the entire house, for sure.

This place is different from anything else I've done, and I'm pretty sure it always will be. It's so quirky, I don't think I could re-create it even if I tried.

OPPOSITE AND PREVIOUS PAGES: The clients here embraced color and pattern with the decorating equivalent of a bear hug, and they brought their own major collection of country-house-cool antiques to the project. The chinoiserie-filled dining room and more relaxed living room show off the results. The poppy accent hues—green in the dining room, pink in the living room—keep things informal.

From the big picture right down to the small details, more was always more in this house. I put colors together in unique combinations and then worked to balance all those hues to get each space to sing. **PREVIOUS PAGES:** The mix of soft greens with bright turquoise accents in the sun porch is one of those unlikely color combos, but it works, and it plays nicely with the pink outdoor furniture just beyond.

ABOVE: More bright colors, which strike a retro 1960s note here, help the laundry room feel groovy.
OPPOSITE: The homeowners and I decided to leave the kitchen largely as we found it since it was in good shape. We only switched out the lights, stools, window treatments, and backsplash. To bring the room to life a bit more, I had the backsplash tiles painted with local plant life, birds, and other animals.

The main bedroom's wallpaper reflects one of the homeowner's love for chinoiserie, as well as her sense of whimsy. The rose and moss colors make it such a happy space. As in most of the house, nearly every piece of furniture is vintage, which is great, because it means almost nothing in this home says, "I know where they bought that!" That's true even of the new pieces, which we reimagined by repainting, refinishing, or recovering—things we did for the antiques, too.

LIFE LESSON

Reimagine, Refinish, Repeat

The owners of this house had a ton of interesting vintage furniture and accessories. They'd been collecting great stuff for decades. Many pieces were heirlooms, which I always love to include in a house, because they feel so special and personal. But some didn't come across as quite right for the playful empty nest that we were now feathering. Luckily, we were able to repurpose much of what they had. How'd we do it? To make these old pieces fit into this new house, we painted or refinished or otherwise reimagined many of the couple's favorite items—including the shield-back chairs in the dining room, the wicker seats in the sunroom, and the antique Herez rug we dusted off for the bedroom here. That's something I do again and again, and you can, too. It just works wonders.

This bedroom toes its way right up to the formal line and is just shy of crossing it before it pulls back. The spiral-columned four-poster bed, the antique carpet, the Edwardian nightstands, the blue-and-white china, even the wall coverings—all classics. Thing is, it all reads as country house classical thanks to the gingham headboard and the color scheme, and that leaves the room relaxed enough to go with the rest of the house.

With its dramatic canopy beds, antique faux-bamboo mirror, and a chinoiserie-painted chest of drawers, this is not your average kids' room, not by a long shot. But you know what? It's one I'd like to stay in. And I'm a kid at heart, so . . . mission accomplished! The devil's in the devilishly good details here, for sure, from the wallpapered ceiling to the patterned contrast borders on the window curtains, bed hangings, and canopies.

New Meets Old

AN ALL-AMERICAN ATMOSPHERE PERFECTLY SUITS A CENTURY-OLD HOUSE REDESIGNED FOR A MODERN FAMILY

The interiors of any home should always be a reflection of its owners. Location, architectural style, and history play a role, too, but that's all secondary. Don't get me wrong: You always try to respect a house's wishes, to listen to what it's telling you it wants to be. But the homeowner's wishes? Those always come first.

Listening to the wants and needs of the people who live there is a big part of what makes this house as relaxed and family-friendly as it is. If I had just listened to the house—which sits in a quiet, picture-perfect suburban neighborhood in central New Jersey—it might have ended up pretty different.

The building itself dates to 1890, and its Victorian style leans toward Queen Anne, thanks to its asymmetry, steeply pitched roof, and wide porch. The tops of the walls in some of the rooms have these great curves up to the ceilings, plus there are amazing diamond-paned windows and some excellent stained-glass doors. Details like these felt like a gift right from the start.

All this hundred-plus-year-old architecture got me thinking in a very formal way. And that's where the family came in. They were anything but formal. The four young kiddos all love to play rough-and-tumble outside, and Mom and Dad both have a pretty relaxed personal style and lifestyle, too, plus a love for the color red and bold stripes (and lots of 'em).

The question for me was how to marry this relaxed-feeling family with the formal architecture of an old house. (Wait, hold up, did I just say I was going to marry the whole family? No, that's not what that says. OK, phew.) I found the answer in an all-American aesthetic that blends the homeowners' cozy, comfortable vibe with their favorite design elements, plus the classic old bones of the house.

To see all this in action, you don't have to look any further than the entry hall. Yeah, I know, just the phrase "entry hall" can seem a little fussy. But this one isn't, I

OPPOSITE AND PREVIOUS PAGES: I've only got one decorating rule that I almost never break: Old houses have to have old things. They just look best that way. Your job is to find ways to make those old things look comfortable to use and modern at the same time. That's exactly what we did in the foyer—and all over—this late-nineteenth-century Victorian house in a drop-dead charming New Jersey suburb.

New York

Like most of the paneling in this house, the family room's wainscoting was darkly painted. Lightening it up enlivened the room and made it right for the family that now chills out in here all the time. In low-key, laid-back spaces like this one, I love to do a big, upholstered ottoman with a tray on top instead of a hard wooden or stone coffee table. Comfort is king!

LIFE LESSON

Fun and Games

When my kids were younger, they loved playing board games. Even more than they loved playing them, however, they seemed to love abandoning them, fully set up and halfway through a game, somewhere in the middle of the family room floor—usually in a spot that was a prime pathway from the kitchen to the sofa, and always with some very sharp playing pieces left for me or my wife to stumble upon. Surprise! And that, my friends, is why, more than board games, I love games tables. Nothing helps get things up off the floor like a place to put those things. Highly recommend, perfect ten outta ten. Paint yours a bold color so the kids can't miss seeing it. It'll function as a reminder—and a warning.

A games table setup is great for any family that loves to sit down and play cards, Scrabble, Guess Who?, you name it. (My favorite was always Sorry!, not sorry about it.) This particular table is just right for the space in front of the window wall. Because this area is also a de facto hallway connecting the foyer to the kitchen, there wasn't enough room for another sofa or other large piece.

promise. We treated its hardwood floors to a playful diamond checkerboard motif, then painted the wainscoting, moldings, and stair balustrades a bright white to lighten things up. Stripes appear in bold red-and-white for the stair runner and then blue-and-white for the wallpaper. That wall covering coordinates with the whimsical fabric chandelier, which looks almost like a leafy potted plant. The furniture here plays up the house's antique character (and there's plenty of furniture, because we wanted this to be a space that really gets used and doesn't just end up as a pass-through). The elegant curves and careful carving of the walnut center table and the petite desk and settee, both with cabriole legs, feel like they're part of the vintage architecture.

And that's key in a century-old house like this, even if you want a relaxed look. This may sound a little, "Well, duh," but when I start an older home, one of my first goals is to get the owners comfortable with antique things. An old house full of new stuff is lame. There is beauty in the mix, to be sure—look at how beautiful that foyer is! The thing is, that mix really needs almost as much old stuff as new for it to work.

The new-old mix, along with the color red and all those stripes, appears again and again in this house, which lets everything hang together from room to room. And that, in turn, helps this family and their guests be totally comfortable hanging out all over.

It doesn't take a lot these days to convince me to tent a ceiling, and here it felt completely natural. The dining room's curving walls just cried out for one. I knew it was a bit of a risk to add the bright blue background of the Roman shades' fabric to the red-outlined subtle greens of the walls, but I balanced things out with seat cushions in a similar aqua hue, so it all ended up simpatico.

The kitchen needed a pretty involved refresh to become the type of light and bright gathering space families want these days. Newly installed but still traditional, it all goes with the Victorian architecture thanks to the crown molding and cabinet profiles, plus the massive range hood and retro-looking range itself, as well as the leaded-glass-fronted upper cabinets. The fun blue and green palette of colorful accents, meanwhile, modernizes everything. As for the huge island, it's an even bigger hit at parties than I am!

Cake Perfection
GENIUS RECIPES
Dinner for Everyone
slow cooker
Walk With Me NEW YORK
NIGEL SLATER
A COOK'S BOOK
75
joy

ABOVE: I'm not really a bath person, but for people who are, you can't beat a soaking tub. Thing is, you have to try them on, almost like they're clothes or a lounge chair, to find the one that fits you juuuuuust right. **OPPOSITE:** To help a color- and pattern-filled space all work together nicely, I like to use the same print in the same color in two or three different ways. In this bedroom, the ticking stripe of the Roman shades and the bed do all the work for you.

RTM

ABOVE AND OPPOSITE: In the same way that red-and-white ticking stripe can bring a bedroom's complex decorating scheme together, red accents used throughout this house make the whole place feel like it's cut from the same cloth—even though there are hundreds of different textiles in the whole thing. (See what I did there? Cloth . . . textiles?) Varying the ways I used that red—in broad swathes some places, as part of a pattern elsewhere—keeps things interesting.

FORMAL

BUT STILL FUN

I grew up in a pretty formal house, with interior designer parents who had a bunch of what we called "five-dollar furniture": sofas and chairs that were so precious—at least to them—that we kids had to pay a five-dollar fine every time we dared to sit in one of them.

We needed to fork over the money even if we didn't have French fry grease or mud-pie mud or unwashable paint on our hands (and we usually did). Now that I'm a designer, too, I've made it my mission to make sure no one has to have any five-dollar furniture. Even precious pieces can be made pretty family-friendly. And I like to think that's true of formal houses, too. They can be fun at the same time.

The thing is, formal all on its own isn't all that fun. And, news flash, it's not what young families are looking for. A lot of them, though, really are looking for an aesthetic that skews toward the traditional.

Often that's because the classical architecture of their house seems to dictate it, or it's what they grew up with or how they entertain, or it's just because they've inherited art and antiques, and that inspires their aesthetic. Even these people usually want their homes to be fun, too.

The key to adding fun is personality. The trick is to fearlessly translate your personality into what your finished home looks like. Formality is safe—with set rules about what you should do and what goes with what. Fun is messier, requiring you to break some rules or at least bend them.

One of the best ways to get the fun going is gathering lots of stuff. It's the more the merrier, within reason, as far as furniture, fabrics, pattern, woodwork, surface treatments, and materials go.

You've also got to think about collections: antiques and art, souvenirs and serving plates, books and blankets, pillows and porcelain. I've created gallery walls of mirrors and family photos, of course, but also displays of golf flags and vintage brackets with various objects on them. The stories behind these pieces are what make an interior special and fun.

Because of this need for stuff, a formal look usually comes easiest to families who've been collecting for a while, or even for generations. But it doesn't have to be that way. Collections that mix eras and styles and places of origin can be gathered, if not overnight, then pretty quickly these days. (Thanks, Internet!)

This collected look looks best when it's the homeowners who take the lead in what to collect. That's the personality part. I can't force a passion for Arts and Crafts pottery on you, and I wouldn't try to, either.

Besides collections, the elements of color and comfort—call them the three Cs—help liven things up. Saturated colors, often in unconventional combinations, give a boost of contrast to an interior, which translates to personality. So, too, do colorful prints and patterns used in surprising, layered ways.

As for comfort, I'm talking about cozy sofas you sink into even if they look like the most tailored thing you've ever seen. I'm talking about antique dining chairs that support your back through dinner. I'm talking about occasional tables always within arm's reach in a living or family room. I'm talking about a hidden bar in the home office. Each lets a formal home be a place you can still have fun in.

In this section, I'll guide you through four houses whose owners were entirely unafraid to infuse their passions and personality into their fairly traditional homes. They did so with collections both new and old, with plenty of color, and with comfort to spare.

At Home with Tradition

CURATING AND COMPLEMENTING THE BEST OF A FAMILY'S HEIRLOOMS

Sometimes, people tell me exactly what they want for their new home. Way more often, though, they show me, and I figure it out from there. Usually, the way they show me is through pictures and links and Instagram and Pinterest. But, if I'm lucky, they show me by inviting me over to see where—and how—they currently live. This is always great.

I remember my first meeting with this homeowner, a young mom, and her school-age sons. I walked into their house and immediately thought, *Man, this is one of the nicest houses I have ever been in.* I knew then and there we had to make their new place a step up from the beautiful home they already had.

What I saw at their current place was a home full of family collections, gathered through generations—and all high-quality and highly traditional pieces. The classic style and the sheer quantity of all that stuff, plus the owner's aesthetic desires, all added up to a formal look for their new place, too.

A collected look came easy to this Lake Forest, Illinois, house. That's because its owner had absolutely incredible family heirlooms: artwork, plates, books, furniture, you name it. I selected a round table for the center of the living room to divide the long, narrow space into two smaller seating areas, and I picked the shades of blue and green from the views outside the windows. **PREVIOUS PAGE:** Details like the foyer's faux leather–wrapped, nailhead-studded stair rail play nicely with the house's antique and vintage pieces. Together, they add up to the level of formality that this family wanted.

I like to use trim tape—like the patterned blue version here—to hide wallpaper seams. It creates a very finished appearance. The tape in this room also helps visually anchor the display of blue-and-white china over the sofa, making it appear ordered and rhythmic. A high cocktail table like this one may seem unusually tall, but it works great for keeping drinks in an easy-to-reach location, and it fits well in this relatively small seating area.

To me, creating a formal space is about a lot of different things. But it's hard to get it right if you don't own pieces that can tell a story. And while you definitely can pull collections together, already having them is a stronger place to start. This family had such a treasure trove, it sometimes felt like all I needed to do was find spots to put things.

Beyond clearly feeling collected, their previous home was comfortable, too, and it also showed that the owner was deeply into decorative details. So I kept one eye on keeping things cozy, and at the same time ensured that no opportunity for adornment slipped by.

For their new home, in the idyllic Chicago suburb of Lake Forest, I had a chinoiserie-style bamboo trellis hand-painted onto the living room's vaulted ceilings. I tented a closet ceiling with rope-trimmed fabric. I had the stair rail wrapped in faux leather and added nailhead trim. I box pleated the chair skirts. I upholstered the doors. No lampshade was left without trim. Seriously. That's not just an expression. (OK, it's not actually an expression either, but shouldn't it be? Let's make it happen.)

With these details, plus the family's collections of blue-and-white porcelain, leather-bound antique books, gilt-framed mirrors, and so much more, the new house took on some truly formal style. And all those lay-

When I first toured this house, the dining room felt less bright than I hoped it would, so we lacquered the ceiling in a soft sky blue to bounce light around. Then I had the chairs custom-made to look like antiques, backing each with trapunto-style quilting. The curtains and lampshades also show off artisanal details, and the red hues pop against the gray tones of the custom wall mural.

LIFE LESSON

Collect First, Decorate Later

You can't rush formal, so this style often appeals most to—and is best for—people who have (or love gathering) extensive collections of furniture and accessories, often developed over generations. If that's you, then you may find you don't exactly need more stuff, but instead help to cull and group together all that you're already lucky enough to own. From there, it's all about embellishment in the final touches: custom shades on antique light fixtures, trim and window dressing details, artisanal paint finishes, and so much more. A house like this also becomes about protecting the finest finery from accident-prone kiddos: laminating fabrics when possible, stain-treating others, replacing old upholstery with performance textiles. Designing display spaces high above prying hands and sticky fingers always helps, too.

Green always looks great with the colors of leather-bound books, so it was for sure the right choice in this study. I had the walls upholstered, lining the edges with trim in a contrasting red that matches the imitation leather–wrapped door. With the antique books, dark wood, and traditional textile patterns, this room could have flipped too serious. I lightened things up with the playful bobbin fringe on the shade of the faux tortoise lamp.

The family room underwent a major transformation. Before I got started, the drywall tray ceiling looked terrible, and the fireplace stones had been painted black. Black! Can you imagine? We immediately had the fireplace whitewashed, and then had decorative painter Bob Christian treat the ceilings with a bamboo trellis motif. And then, just like that, the space was ready for the overstuffed traditional upholstery we brought in, plus the sisal carpet, bamboo shades, and fun prints that remove any hint of stuffiness.

AGO 1871-1921
E D'ORSAY
AI
BARRON & LARCHER
GROOM
Impressionism, Fashion, & Modernity

ers of detail help the collections seem like they've always been here—they look perfectly at home.

Upstairs in the boys' territory, formal gives way to a cozier, fun vibe—in the media room, say, with its corner sofas and striped walls. But this is still probably the most serious house I have ever done. The level of detail, quality, and craft here works well for this family because the kids are used to it, which wouldn't be true for everyone. These boys have never known anything different. Here, I didn't see the need to use outdoor fabric to cover every stitch of upholstered furniture like I usually do in a home with small kids. Her sons could be trusted (mine, not so much.)

In the end, the style of the house jibes not just with this family, but with what Lake Forest is all about: It's put together and grounded in tradition, tailored but also comfortable, and very, very welcoming. This trio found a town that perfectly matches the way they like to live, and I was happy to make a space for them that matched it—and them—too.

Details matter in every house, but especially here, where the level of finishes, embellishments, and accessories needed to keep pace with the owner's vintage and antique heirlooms. Her collections required a complementary setting. And that's exactly what we gave them. Just some of the highlights? A bathroom featuring gilded lamp shades on sconces and another with a felt-upholstered ceiling; pleated, fringed, and nailhead trims; and a custom embroidered border on the leading edge of floor-length curtains.

Rather than going through the time and effort—not to mention expense—of gutting the whole kitchen and designing a new one, we just did a brightly colored wash on the cabinets, which had been darkly stained. This made them look antiqued and the furthest thing from generic. The room is now the central hangout space for the whole house, used as much for homework as family meals.

1797

ABOVE: The mudroom's got vinyl wallpaper, so it's virtually indestructible, while the custom locker-style cabinets have screened fronts to allow for airflow that keeps things fresh inside and out. I hung the owner's framed collection of vintage *New Yorker* covers facing the lockers. **OPPOSITE:** Things got extra cheery in the laundry room, which doubles as a home office. The fun color, botanical wallpaper, and fringed curtains disguise the fact that this was once a closet.

The owner brought the upholstered headboard in her bedroom from her previous home. I had a canopy made in the same pattern to help the bed look like it had always been here. **FOLLOWING PAGES:** The owner's boys have bedrooms that continue the highly patterned, colorful, and antique-filled aesthetic of the rest of the house, but in younger, more playful ways.

HOUZARD
DRAGON
GARDE NATIONAL
GENIUS AT WORK

Formal Goes Funky

A YOUNG COUPLE TAKE COLOR AND PATTERN TO NEW HEIGHTS

You all know I'm not really a fancy-pants guy. I just play one on Instagram, and not even all that well. So this apartment—in a classic, limestone-clad prewar building on Chicago's Lake Shore Drive with awesome views of Lake Michigan—got me excited to expand my fancy-pants persona. But it also got me a bit nervous. Would all my fancy-pants acting abilities be enough to cut it here, not just in a fancy-pants building, but in my first fancy-pants big-city project? Have I said fancy-pants too much yet? No? Fancy-pants, fancy-pants, fancy-pants!

MYKONOS
CAPRI DOLCE VITA

ABOVE, OPPOSITE, AND PREVIOUS PAGES: To get this Chicago home's living and dining areas to feel separate but connected, I used a pair of twinned rugs to define each zone, plus matching curtains, cabinets, and mirrors. Other than that, I changed the fabrics and colors from one area to the other. And what colors and fabrics they are! Nothing was too bold for the fun, young homeowners here. **PAGE 108:** We embraced the darkness of the windowless foyer with a deep blue wall covering.

As it turns out I had no reason to be scared. And that was all due to this apartment's owners, a young couple moving from a cozy one bedroom elsewhere in the city to this 4,500-square-foot, seventh-floor four bedroom. One half of the couple had grown up in this very building, which could have upped the pressure on me even more. But it didn't because both she and her husband didn't want any whiff of old-school formality. In fact, they pushed me—me, a guy who knows no limits!—to think bigger and bolder when it came to color and pattern and how both together help the whole thing seem somewhat formal but not stuffy. Thanks to them, I think we created something pretty special here.

The apartment already had its own formal point of view in the form of character-rich architectural details: wainscot panels in almost every room and great ceiling beams throughout. I wanted the decorating to be just as interesting to stand up to all this and, at the same time, turn the formality down a couple notches. Luckily, the homeowners were more than game and not at all afraid to take chances.

The amount of color they were ready for in the larger spaces here? That's not something most people would be comfortable with. Usually, more than three or four hues in a room is where I start to lose people.

In relatively formal rooms, I always like to design in elements that encourage everyday use. That way, these spaces don't sit empty. Here, a TV pops up out of the cabinet in the living area, and the matching one by the dining table serves as a bar. As for the mirrors, they help bounce light around to the walls that don't have windows with Lake Michigan views.

But these homeowners weren't that way. If a curtain fabric I showed them had six or seven different colors in it—like the one we ended up using in the main living and dining area—they wanted that.

They also wanted patterns that spoke to them and told a story, and they took any opportunity to lean into more color, and in bolder hues, too. If I showed them a "safe" scheme, and then a "risky" one, they never chose safe. And that's what prevents this place from getting fussy or fusty.

The other thing that helps is a sense of comfort. Even though the couple didn't have any kids when we started working together, they were planning to, and, sure enough, they had a baby soon after they moved in. (The office became a nursery.) It was important to them as a young family—the same way it always is to me, as a dad of two wild kids—that everything felt accessible. Every piece of seating here welcomes you to plop down on it; every table will be OK if you put your feet up on it; and every room has a real, everyday purpose that tempts you to use it.

In an urban apartment, even one this big, you're limited on space, so my main goal was to get the most out of every single room. I did that by giving people a reason to go into each.

Consider the shared main dining and living area. I painted the coffers in the high

I had to rip out the grand dining room in this apartment—whose building dates to the 1920s—to create space for the type of open-plan, entertaining-ready kitchen contemporary families love. It hurt, but it was worth it. This gathering, cooking, and snacking spot now fills the old kitchen area and half the old dining room, with the other half serving as a new family room.

ABOVE: A leather-upholstered door finished with nailhead trim serves as the icing on the cake in this sweet little powder room. **OPPOSITE:** The home's breakfast area occupies a cozy—if not downright tight—back room of the house with basically no view. I made the most of the situation by picking a botanical wallpaper that would give you something to look at. It helps you imagine you're in a quiet courtyard garden in the middle of the city.

Even in an apartment that almost explodes with pattern and color, this room is out there, which is just what the homeowners wanted. This space exists away from the rest of the home, so I realized we could majorly go for it. And we did. Since the wallpaper has such a complicated motif, I used mostly solids, albeit bright ones for the rest of the pieces. The armchair is the only major exception, but its organic print meshes well with the more graphic walls.

ceiling in two shades of green to keep the room from feeling too grand. That also gave it more human scale by making the ceiling appear lower. And I used rugs to define the separate sitting and eating areas, which helps each one read as an intimate space you truly want to be in. The furniture does the same. Nearly every piece features soft, embracing curves and eclectic colors and prints. And I designed user-friendly details like a hidden bar in one cabinet and a TV in another.

In our early conversations, the homeowners said "funky" a lot when describing what they wanted. And we tried to get that sensibility into the design. Maybe at the end of the day this place is as much about putting the funky in formal as it is about adding the fun. Funky and fun—the two go hand in hand here. No fancy-pants required.

There's so much going on in these spaces, and many of the prints and pieces lean contemporary. But careful construction and considered embellishments keep the overall look formal, traditional, and on point. **PAGE 124:** I like to go gender neutral in a guest bedroom, skipping color or using colors that aren't obviously gendered. Here, I went with a bit of both boys-like-blue and girls-like-pink stereotypes. **PAGE 125:** Always try to get a sofa in a home office. You're as likely to work on your laptop there as at a desk these days.

MODERN MIX
36

LIFE LESSON

Flexible Family, Flexible Space

You may not be able to tell by looking at it, which is kind of the point, but this sweet little nursery began its young life as an office, and it will become one again someday after the baby who currently calls it home—and any future siblings—have moved on to a big-kid bedroom. The homeowners and I wanted the transition from office to nursery and back to office to be relatively seamless, without requiring a major redo (and then another one). So we went with neutrals and avoided anything that read as too cute or too juvenile. This may sound strange, but in some ways, we didn't think about designing the nursery just as a baby's room, because it had to be more flexible than that. The botanical fabric window treatments, for example, made just as much sense and looked just as good when this was an office and will still be right if this space eventually becomes a guest room, too. Nurseries are temporary, so for anything permanently installed, we decorated with Mom in mind, thinking about her moving back in with her laptop and desk someday. All the baby stuff is temporary and easy to remove.

This baby nursery—and former home office—is a totally peaceful escape from the bustling city you can see right outside. The clear-skies blue hue on the walls, the super-soft ivory rug and rocker, and the springtime-y green and pink floral Roman shades make any stress fly out those corner windows.

LAPINS

Fancy and Fanciful

AN ART-FILLED, ENTERTAINING-READY HOME FOR A CREATIVE FAMILY WITH THREE SCHOOL-AGE GIRLS

To give you just a tiny bit of an idea of the mega scale of this big but still very homey feeling home, think about this: There is a sitting area in the main bathroom. (No, not that kind of sitting area. Get your mind out of the . . . gutter.)

Yeah, anyway, we had a lot to work with here, which is great, and not just because of all that space. This place also got my designer juices flowing thanks to its impressive, classical interior details, which came courtesy of the team at the Miami firm Portuondo Perotti Architects, who designed this new-build, Georgian-inspired home. Those traditional elements definitely pointed this place in a more formal direction. Then there was the collection of brightly hued, large-scale contemporary art brought to the project by the homeowners, one of whom is a talented artist herself.

AMERICAN FASHION
CUBA

I also grooved on the location, right on a sparkling blue lake surrounded by lush greenery in Coral Gables, just outside of Miami. That lent the house this tropical forest atmosphere that culitvated throughout.

Besides the art collection, the owners had an endless appetite for the color blue, a hunger I definitely shared with them. They also had an open mind about giving the rooms different decorating themes. Because you can't see from one space into another here, we felt free to change things up between them. The level of design and detail results in an enticing sense of discovery and surprise from room to room—and within each, too.

It all still looks very put together, however, as a formal home should, and that was right for the sensibility of these owners: a husband-and-wife couple with great taste and three daughters who are now teenagers. But at the same time, this house is just one of those places where you want to wander around and discover new things, which provides that sense of fun.

At this sweeping South Florida home, statement-making art from the clients' collection makes their living room stand out. Putting a portrait by the games table lets it seem almost as if a third person is playing. **PREVIOUS PAGES:** A graphic rug works best when you make it either the largest or smallest pattern in a room.

Every space gives you a lot to take in—not too much, but a lot. I like to think the whole thing is a little *Where's Waldo?* because, if you search (and you'll want to in these rooms), you can always find something new and interesting. It could be a playful detail in the hand-painted mural in the bar, the artisanal finish of the lampshades in the living room, or the tape-trimmed scallops of the curtain valance in one of the daughter's bedrooms.

All these hidden Easter eggs make the house a ton of fun for guests, which is excellent and something I was definitely thinking about while we were designing, because this family loves to entertain. This place was built—and then decorated—for parties.

Check out the living room: It has three separate sitting areas, which I defined with a trio of sofa setups, placing them so guests would never have their backs to each other. This room alone has more than a dozen different blue patterns in it, most of them all in a similar shade, which helps them work together. And it's the better for it. Additional color comes from the outstanding, eye-catching art on the walls.

That's pretty true throughout the house. It's the art that brings the brightest and most unexpected combinations of colors. Otherwise, each room doesn't have

LIFE LESSON

Art Matters

If you're someone with a collection of large-scale artwork—whether paintings or sculptures or both—you want to design your home around these pieces from the get-go. In the case of this new-build house, done for a couple of contemporary art collectors (the wife herself is an artist) and their daughters, we found a place in the floor plan for every major piece before ground was even broken on construction. Also key here is that it's the art, rather than a cool rug or wall covering or lead fabric, that gets to be the thing that sets the tone for each room. From there, the furnishings needed to be interesting enough, but the art remains the star.

In a relatively long, narrow kitchen, you're likely to end up with a long, narrow island. When that happens, I find it works nicely to let one end of it become a stand-in for a dining table. **PREVIOUS PAGES:** Furnishings representing a range of different styles and eras give the dining room a sense of timelessness.

more than two real colors in it, sometimes even just one, like in the living room. And that's OK.

In this house, the limited use of different colors in one room was partially about the owners, who weren't into the idea of layering with many hues, but it's also about a level of formality. Generally—and you'll see me break this rule in this book—the fewer colors you use in a room, the more formal it can be. Or, at least, the easier it is to keep it feeling formal.

The dining room barely uses any color, except for the blue linen–upholstered chairs. But it still manages to lean into the tropics. A custom sepia-hued botanical mural, rather than one featuring more expected, brightly hued flora, covers every wall.

In the bar, meanwhile, I took inspiration from the colors of a Gucci scarf I'd seen, combining soft and dark taupe shades with the Italian fashion house's signature green. The room's grass cloth–covered walls bring in some texture and further soften the formality. To me, that material is all you need to take a traditionally wood-trimmed room like this one and make it seem much more approachable.

A local painter delivered a finishing touch of whimsy to the walls surrounding the bar shelving by creating an immersive tropical mural, this one in shades of green, with various blue and pink accents, plus a few finely feathered parrots that I just couldn't resist having him add. It's all in a day's squawk—I mean, a day's work—for me.

OPPOSITE AND PREVIOUS PAGES: A Gucci scarf I'd seen inspired the bar room's palette of green and neutral hues. The main lounging space here is pretty put together and buttoned up, but it's a whole different story when you turn to the bar. There, a playful, parrot-dotted, hand-painted mural surrounds the antique mirror–backed white oak shelves.

ABOVE AND OPPOSITE: When you look at them side by side like this, these two bedrooms illustrate a great decorating truth. Saturated colors tend to play well with other saturated colors, while lighter shades tend to do best with other pastels. **PREVIOUS PAGES:** I took a break from all the blue to design the main suite as a place apart. I love how the bed alcove left plenty of room for a really comfortable and inviting living area.

I became involved with this house early enough in its construction that I got to select the tiles that line its oval pool. I went with pink because it provides a flash of contrast against all the tropical greenery and because it felt like a nod to the 1960s and '70s parties you might see in classic Slim Aarons photos—just the sort of gatherings I could see the homeowners hosting. As a bonus, the color also matches the flamingos that wade in the neighboring lake.

FAMILY EST. 2004

A Kid-Friendly Showplace

A SUBURBAN CONNECTICUT WEEKEND HOME BECOMES A FANTASTICAL PRIMARY RESIDENCE FOR A FAMILY OF FIVE

Even for me, a guy who thinks you can't spell "formal" without "fun" (hey, spelling was never my strong suit), it's a rare thing to create a house that's as classically put together as this one and still have it be fun. I need to give a lot of the credit for that to the homeowners, a husband and wife and their three school-age daughters. They wanted to take some risks here in order to create something decidedly unique.

The wife especially—whose personal style mixes the tailored traditionalism of Lee Radziwill with the loose, carefree look of the main character's costuming in a Nancy Meyers movie—was into lots of color, and her aesthetic drove this project.

The owners of this Connecticut home wanted a house that didn't look like anyone else's, and they wanted a sense of surprise, and they wanted to show they weren't afraid of color and pattern. (Just the opposite, in fact.) The living room started with the wallpaper, which feels formal even though it's whimsical, because of the traditional architecture. I then had to pick all the other pieces in the room to keep pace with that paper—and boy, do they. **PREVIOUS PAGE:** We left the foyer bright and open as a break between the moodier living and dining rooms.

The other big-idea info I got from the family, who lived primarily in Manhattan and planned to use this Connecticut home mostly on weekends, was that they hoped this house would transport them to another place, and a surprising one, too. They wanted a fun, fanciful design that grabbed your attention as soon as you walked in—one that made you feel like you'd truly escaped and left behind not only the stress of the city, but that of the entire real world, too.

This project was a rarity for another reason, too. While homeowners and I usually work together to decorate an entire house all at once, we worked on this one room by room over five years, starting with the formal dining room. There, the client wanted to use a trip she'd taken to India as inspiration. She'd been blown away by the aesthetic in Rajasthan, especially the often-fantastical design of its Mughal palaces and the beautiful hand-block prints that local artisans have specialized in for centuries.

You can totally see echoes of these in the custom mural hand-painted on the walls. Its silhouetted creatures add a whole bunch of whimsy to the traditionalism of the woodwork and the regal furniture. (There's a tiered, leaded-crystal chandelier and painted Swedish-style chairs.) The straightforward blue-and-white palette, meanwhile, balances out any old-school fustiness.

I especially love the living room's corner sectional, which helps take the edge off any formality. It's just a total kick-off-your-shoes, sit-on-down piece of furniture. The whole setting is wonderfully transporting, too, which is something else the owners wanted from their home. This nook sends you on a warm-weather vacation—something you definitely need during cold New England winters.

Once the dining room set the tone, we wanted each of the main floor's entertaining spaces to take you on just as beautiful a journey, but to other places. So the breakfast room, for example, became a British Georgian-style orangery, its mural-like wall covering of blossoms and boughs reaching for the latticework ceiling.

The living room came last, but it ended up first in our hearts. Once we fell in love with the secret garden wall mural paper, everything fell into place. We never quite figured out where in the world the room is meant to be, but we know for sure it's the place that everyone wants to be in the house.

The old-new, formal-fun mix is what makes that the case, I think. You've got this grand but somehow graphic wallpaper; a candelabra-style chandelier, but in a vivid teal; and antique and contemporary furniture—including big, gracious, comfortable sofas—that wouldn't be out of place in an English country house. We had them all upholstered in bright fabrics and contrasting patterns.

Doing each room one by one made it a little bit of a challenge to get the flow right. But it all worked out in the end. The consistent traditional-eclectic aesthetic mix lets that happen. Then, each space has a statement wallpaper or curtain fabric or saturated color that takes the lead in the design.

The owner had great memories of a trip to Jaipur, India, and asked me to design the dining room to reflect the woodblock prints she'd been drawn to there. Decorative painter Bob Christian created a mural that does that very thing. The Rajasthani surroundings keep company with an impressive crystal chandelier, creating a whole Mughal palace look. Could have ended up real, real formal, I know. Keeping things light—in this case mostly white—and all done in just two colors makes it fun.

Finally, I always like rooms to proceed from lighter to darker when you walk or look through them from the front door. I ensured that happened here.

The homeowners originally intended to use this as a second home, but once it was completed, they loved it so much they made it their primary. And that makes sense to me, if I do say so myself. When I look back on this project, the biggest thing I remember is how many great ideas we put into each room to help it become the perfect haven for this family.

In this house, the sense of levity emerges in the charming details. Lacquering the traditional dining room chairs' legs white instead of darkly stained brown brings them into the twenty-first century, while a contrast fabric on the back of an upholstered chair contributes a playful peekaboo element. The very verdant wallpaper above blue-painted beadboard wainscoting in a bathroom looks like a privet hedge peeking up over the top of a picket fence, and painting the homeowners' previously brown antique dining chairs a distressed gunmetal gray lets them seem new again. I find that powder rooms are the best place to go all in with wallpaper, and I love that even the tabletop items in this house have a bit of a fantasy forest look.

The kitchen was in great shape when the owners bought the house, so we decided to leave it basically untouched. Its all-white look let us have that much more fun in the surrounding rooms. Still, this space did need something to punch it up. We found that something in the deep salmon hue used on the barstools' upholstery.

Another transporting spot in the house is the breakfast room, which I turned into the sort of orangery you might see at a Georgian estate in the British countryside. See how I carried the salmon color from the wall covering into the cushions on the kitchen barstools and the dining chairs? That helps the whole room look super sophisticated, but, at the same time, it's got an outdoor rug and vinylized fabric, so you could basically spray the whole thing down with a hose to clean it.

ABOVE AND OPPOSITE: This is what you do when you're tired of your dark wood–paneled study: You reinvent it as a sitting room and reenergize it with some high-gloss paint. (If you ever want the wood grain back, you can always just have it sanded and re-stained. Easy!)

Can you tell this kid likes pink? She told me it was her favorite, and I decided we'd give her every shade of the color we could find. I used the floral artwork to pull most of the specific hues. **PREVIOUS PAGES:** The owners' bedroom is a classic example of one of my favorite tricks: using a bold lead fabric to create your color palette. The pattern we picked for the window treatments gave me all the hues I needed for everything else here.

LIFE LESSON

It's a Kids' World

It doesn't take a genius to tell you that your children's bedrooms and play spaces should be designed for them. But it's a smart move to have these areas designed *by* them, too. I'm not suggesting you let them loose with a can of paint and a glue gun and say "Have at it." Far from it. Instead, I'm thinking more about your letting them pick colors and inspirations. That way, you can keep the family peace and prevent the whole thing from leading with *Paw Patrol* prints. Consider giving a few choices for the main fabric or wallpaper or the rug that will guide the overall design and color choices. Or start by talking about the color or colors your kiddo wants in their space. That's how it worked in this house, where one daughter loved aqua and lavender and the other two loved pink. To keep the pink rooms from looking too similar, we went with a punchy version of the hue in one and a more subtle one in the other, matching the girls' personalities. For all three, we taped a bunch of different wallpapers up and made sure the children had a chance to weigh in on which they preferred. Then, by using the lead color in each room in different patterns and textures, we managed to work in the formality found in the rest of the house. That monochromatic mix gave the rooms a maturity that the girls could grow into, too, which was just as important.

I updated this children's room, where the owners already had placed the beds and built-ins, by adding the pale rug, the bold ceiling wallpaper, and the curving benches at the foot of the bed. The infusion of color and pattern gives a big dose of kid-friendly liveliness to the space.

NEUTRAL

BUT STILL EXCITING

OK, let's get this out of the way right away and address the beige elephant in the room: I am not known as a neutral guy. Sure, in my designs, you'll see some ecru here, some ivory there. But I mostly use these to set off saturated colors and vibrant patterns. The eye needs a break, after all. (There are no elephants in any of the spaces in these pages. Sorry to disappoint you.)

That said, I love an entirely neutral interior, and many of the families whose houses I design do, too. Believe it or not, in real life, I'm less in-your-face dramatic than you may think. So I can relate when someone tells me they don't want their home to be all hopped up on color and pattern.

Often, people request a neutral scheme because they want the decorating to recede so they can emphasize something else: amazing architecture, views, or art. All great reasons, but your house doesn't need any of those to justify going neutral. It's enough to just want your home to feel peaceful and restful and warm, which neutral does extremely well.

Here's the funny thing, though: Unlike other looks, this neutral one isn't always about your style or personality. I've done colorful primary residences for high-energy families and then gone way neutral for their weekend getaways. Those vacation retreats are where they go to relax. Often, they also have stunning views. And that means beige for the win.

It makes a lot of sense, if you think about it. When you go to a spa, the chances of encountering a wildly colorful scheme are slim to none, and that's because you're supposed to find peace there. Soft colors and textures with subtle patterns have a calming effect. Not that you can't relax in a brightly hued home, but colorful rooms exude excitement while neutral ones are designed to truly relax in. Their atmosphere can still be happy, but in a quieter way. If I had my druthers—and unlimited resources—I would order one of each, please, with a cherry on top, because I like both feelings.

The good news is that you don't have to pick one or the other. A neutral interior can be both calming and a bit exciting. The trick is to mix materials and provide just enough visual interest. When going neutral, I love to combine natural wood and stone with nubby, woven, and even furry fabrics and textiles. I use small-scale prints on large pieces (curtains, say, or a sofa) and large-scale prints for accents (like throw pillows). All these materials also bring the warmth, which is important, because neutral interiors can easily seem cold.

Here are a few other traps that can be easy to fall into: First, not all neutrals naturally go together, because not every beige is the same. Each one will have a hint of a color behind it—one may tint toward green, another toward purple. You need to find tones that all tint in the same direction.

Next, there's not much leeway. For a spare palette to work, it's got to be carefully considered. To check, review your swatches and other samples together under natural light and lamplight in the rooms where you plan to use them.

One more element to keep in mind: Neutral rooms need a statement-making feature to prevent things from getting snoozy. In contrast to a formal interior, a neutral one doesn't need a lot of stuff to make a statement. Often, in fact, the less the better, which is why these sorts of spaces work well in modern, contemporary, or minimalist architecture.

But enough talk. Let's get down to business and show you neutral in (subtle, quiet) action in the four houses here.

Letting the View Shine

A NORTH CAROLINA LAKE HOUSE GETS A TEXTURE-RICH SCHEME FOR A COUPLE WITH TWO GROWN CHILDREN

I'm a sweatpants kind of guy. I don't wear them in public . . . not all that often anyway. But I do love them. No surprise there, right? But it may come as a surprise—especially given my fondness for sweatpants—that this super-stylish lake house got its start in a super-stylish outfit. Don't worry, though. It wasn't something I'd picked out to put on myself.

During one of my early meetings with one of the homeowners here—whose family I'd designed two previous houses for, in Florida and the Bahamas—she said, "I want this house to look the way I'm dressed."

I looked more closely at her and immediately realized she had a very good point. She had on some fur, some leather, some cotton, some wool—all natural materials with plenty of soft, interesting texture, and all in neutral hues that blended together beautifully. Everything looked comfortable, clean-lined, and perfectly tailored for her. I knew then that the house could do the same, and I got really into discovering all the possibilities of a neutral scheme.

The homeowner's clothing wasn't the only thing that made a neutral scheme right for this house, however. There was also its lakeside setting in the mountains of North Carolina, with incredible views through huge windows of the surrounding forest, and in every season, too. How could I compete with the rich reds, oranges, and yellows of autumn, the greens and blues of summer, the icy whites of winter? I mean, I would have figured it out. But why would I *want* to compete with them? Instead, I realized I should just let the interiors stand back so that the landscape could take center stage.

The wild woodland setting did help point me to the mix of textures and natural materials I used here, even if it didn't exactly give me my color scheme, other than the soft blues that echo those of the lake. The rustic surroundings, together with the modern-cabin look of the house's exposed wood-beam architecture, inspired me to combine hard, smooth surfaces—like richly grained white oak, burnished and blackened metals, glazed clay tiles, and honed limestone—with soft wools, linens, cottons, faux fur, raffia, and string, plus leather, suede, and alpaca. It's a mixed assortment, but I tied it all together by using a teeny tiny range of neutral hues.

That textural and material mix gives this neutral scheme a big part of its excitement. The rest comes from the fact that this is a big ole, comfortable, rough-and-tumble family fun house. Together with her husband, the homeowner has two sons, who were both college age when the house was designed. So this is a mountain compound of sorts, designed for a crowd of friends and (ever-expanding) family to stay over. There's a great bar and a pool table, a

OPPOSITE AND PREVIOUS PAGES: Modern as it is, the architecture of this North Carolina lake house takes its inspiration from the surrounding woodlands, and my design for its interiors does the same, mixing rough-hewn natural materials, cozily textured woven textiles, neutral hues, and the beautiful shades of blue seen out on the lake from the home's huge windows.

VOGUE

ABOVE: Relatively sleek modern and contemporary artwork always looks good over a piece of furniture with some texture. **OPPOSITE:** The great room's furnishings mostly take a back seat to the amazing views, and that's just fine with me. Low-slung seating and a subtle, consistent palette of atmospheric tans, grays, and blues was all it took to keep the focus where it should be.

ABOVE: There was almost no unused wall space in the butler's pantry, so I worked in a favorite plaid wallpaper on the ceiling, aka the fifth wall of any room. **OPPOSITE:** I kept the kitchen simple and modern, with a spare palette of marble, hand-glazed Zellige tiles, and warm, honey-toned woods. Using slightly different shades of stain for the floor, ceiling beams, wall cabinets, and island suggests the variation of Mother Nature.

This room has a television in it, but it also has these epic views. I like to think that putting so many chairs around the coffee table, which makes it hard for everyone to see the screen, encourages people to have great conversations instead of just looking at the TV.

playful bunk room, plus plenty of outdoor living areas that make it easy to access the water. You've got large, wide-open spaces—like the double-height living room, ready to seat a dozen plus people—for everyone to pile into together, and then smaller ones, too, including a cozy, library-like study, for folks to escape to as needed.

When I started this house, I was psyched, but I also thought that neutrals would never have the instant wow factor that big, dramatic pattern does. By the time I finished, though, I found that's more of a first-impression thing. There's no obvious "look at me" element—other than that view (and look at *that view!*), which is the whole point. But once you spend time in these rooms, you realize the textures, subtle patterns, finishes, cool hardware, and other little details all up the ante and add up to something that's just as interesting, just as enticing, as maximalist color and pattern.

ABOVE: This house's views led me to tone down the decorating. Here in the main bathroom, I used just white and light gray. **OPPOSITE:** This guest bedroom enjoys maybe the best panoramas in the house. I had the curtains here—and throughout the home—mounted further out past the edges of the windows than I usually would. That means that when they're open, as much glass as possible is exposed so you can see more of the forested surroundings.

It's amazing to me that just ten or so years ago, no one had ever, ever asked me for a bunk room in a house. And now? Nearly every homeowner I work with has to have one. I totally get why: They're cozy and comfortable, they maximize additional sleeping space while taking up minimal room, and kids love 'em. This one, with its queen-size beds, works for adults, too—though I'd still opt for that corner guest room, if I were you.

GRAY MALIN

LIFE LESSON

Take It Outside

When you're looking to erase almost any distinction between indoors and out—and that's something I find more and more homeowners are hoping their houses can do these days—then huge expanses of glass can do wonders. Just look at what they do in this house! But even without that sort of architecture (which, let's face it, sadly, most of us aren't lucky enough to have), there's a lot you can do to bring the outdoors in and vice versa. Borrow your palette of colors, materials, and textures directly from your surroundings. Hang curtains and shades to sit entirely outside of the windows' glass to maximize light and views. Or—stick with me here—forgo window treatments entirely in spaces where they may not be necessary, like a living or dining room. Lastly, be sure to turn outside spaces into alfresco rooms using comfortable furniture that looks like it could be inside and that continues the style and colors of your interior scheme.

OPPOSITE AND FOLLOWING PAGES: Space for outdoor cooking, dining, and lounging is a must-have at a lake house. **PREVIOUS PAGES:** Because this games room is on the lower level—with good views, but not the great ones found above—it seemed the perfect spot to break away from soft and subtle neutrals and go a bit more glam with a mirrored bar, fur pillows, and mod chandelier and pool table. I love it all, and so do the homeowners.

Eclectic European Style

A MID-TWENTIETH-CENTURY-INSPIRED PALM BEACH HOME THAT'S EQUAL PARTS MUSEUM-QUALITY AND KID-FRIENDLY

If this house looks different from all the other neutral ones in this section—maybe even different from all the other houses in this book—you're not seeing things. It *is* different. The homeowners here wanted something pretty unique from a lot of other people who come to me for help. They were looking for rooms that would be family-friendly and fun, for sure, but they also asked me to take inspiration from the swank art deco and mid-century designs of France and Italy. These styles mixed modern and classic in entirely new ways, and as a result, this project took me in an entirely new direction.

The couple also wanted to incorporate their expanding collection of contemporary art, their interest in vintage twentieth-century furnishings, and passion for exquisite pieces of stone. So, even though this house ended up with a somewhat reserved color scheme—the better to show off the art and all the custom and vintage pieces—there's nothing neutral about the place.

The design here blends classic with modern, old with new, and the precious with the indestructible. More than any other house I've designed, this one approaches museum quality. But, at the same time, the kids can still enjoy free run of (almost) the entire place. It turns out, even in a museum, indoor-outdoor performance fabrics and other tried-and-true durable materials do the trick.

For me, the first sign this would be no ordinary house, and that the owners were not my ordinary clients, came shortly after architect Daniel Kahan, of the top-flight South Florida studio Smith & Moore, suggested me for the project. I learned they were looking for sophisticated but eclectic interiors for the grand, modern, and classically influenced limestone and stucco house they were planning in Palm Beach.

After meeting the owners, I started getting emails from them with pictures of incredible stone they'd put on reserve: all huge slabs and massive quantities. Thanks to this serious appetite for marbles and travertines, we were able to use stone in major (and majorly surprising) ways—as wainscoting in the main bathroom, for example, and to clad every wall from floor to ceiling in the spa, but then also to form an entire vanity in a powder room, as well as the whole of the kitchen island. There's nothing neutral about any of that.

The richness and quality of the other materials and finishes had to keep pace with the architecture and this impressive use of stone. So we searched out exquisite and richly grained teak and rosewood mid-century modern furniture to use throughout; we designed a custom plaster-relief ceiling for the daughter's room; we had a pair of sofas upholstered in cashmere (cashmere!) for the great room; and we commissioned custom mural papers for many of the walls.

OPPOSITE AND PREVIOUS PAGES: Among my favorite artisanal, spare-no-expense details in this mid-century-modern-meets-neoclassical South Florida tour de force? The foyer floor's marble Greek key border, which takes turn after turn around the room. A foyer scheme as neutrally hued as this one needed some major art to make a statement, so, above a 1940s French art deco sideboard, I hung a Charles Arnoldi work the owners acquired.

I don't wanna toot my own horn . . . OK, maybe I do just a little. But isn't this just the greatest of great rooms? From the mantel carved from a single block of Italian Calacatta cognac marble to the custom sofas upholstered in cashmere and the pale blue chairs by modernist icon Gio Ponti, this space is just—I'll say it again—great. That mantel had to take center stage, so we chose a relatively quiet artwork by Sandy Ostrau to go over it.

ABOVE: If you haven't been able to figure this out by now, I'll tell you: The owners of this house had amazing taste, a love of the finest details, and a fierce fascination with marble and other stone. For this powder room, we encased the entire vanity in bronze-inlaid lilac-veined Turkish marble. **OPPOSITE:** The great room also serves as the house's semiformal dining area. The gypsum-fronted cabinets with straw marquetry mirrors hanging above invite you through double pocket doors to the family room.

THE CARTIER COLLECTION

Those wallpapers also helped us introduce color in artisanal ways here and there, which was important. Even in the most neutral schemes, you need to break up all that beige. In almost every space in this home, we found a place for a pop of color. In the back kitchen, it's high-gloss emerald green on all the cabinets. In the main bedroom, a barely there powder blue on the settee.

All in, this house is a great example of how, when you have amazing architecture, you may find that neutral interiors are just what you want. You know I love color more than anyone—it can be your best friend. Something it's incredibly good at is hiding a lack of existing architecture, or at least a lack of *good* existing architecture. But that's not something this house suffered from. It had good, no, *great*, architecture, and in spades. That meant we needed to dial back the bold color and the big patterns, to guarantee that the interiors were complementing the architecture, not distracting from it.

From its smallest accessories to its grandest light fixtures, this house all but overflows with impressive antique finds and custom contemporary creations. As we gathered everything together, we put a big focus on selecting textures that would simultaneously coordinate and contrast with each other. That's one of the best ways to create interest in a neutral color scheme. So you've got beautifully glazed vintage pottery and ceramics, sleek boxes and other objects by art deco bigwig René Lalique, richly grained white oak parquet floors that wouldn't be out of place in a Paris pied-à-terre, a console clad in translucent slices of selenite stone, a parchment-covered coffee table, and, not least of all, an absolutely epic six-foot-by-six-foot tiered crystal chandelier that dangles from the double-height foyer's skylight.

One of the more relaxed spaces in a pretty tightly tailored and formal house, the kitchen remains sophisticated. We made the whole island out of marble here—to suit the owners' style—rather than just using stone for the countertop. That marble cladding, and its angular, asymmetrical shape, give the island a sculptural, contemporary look that balances the more traditional detailing of the rest of the room.

ABOVE AND OPPOSITE: It's the rare house where a main kitchen takes something of a back seat to the butler's pantry, but this house is pretty much a unicorn, so I figured if not here, where, and if not now, when? The stone-loving owners found the riotously veined slabs of Calacatta Borghese marble at their favorite stone showroom, and we leaned into its purples and gray greens by pairing it with green-lacquered brass-inlaid cabinets and a green leather–upholstered door.

ABOVE AND OPPOSITE: The joint family room and breakfast area feel entirely in keeping with the rest of this ultra-luxe house, even though I designed them with the owners' young kids in mind. Pale neutral colors notwithstanding, this room is pretty indestructible thanks to a ton of performance textiles and hardwood furniture. These cushions and pillows won't stain no matter how greasy and saucy the slice of pizza that lands cheese-side-down on them, and the other furniture, as well as the floors, are majorly scratch- and chip-resistant.

ABOVE AND OPPOSITE: I'm always keeping track of new decorating concepts I have and looking for the right house to use them in—which is something you can do, too, so you have an ideas file to return to when you're ready to do some redesigning. I'd been thinking about the combed crosshatch pattern I had painted on the walls here for a while, and when I saw the millwork that architect Daniel Kahan had come up with for the main bedroom, I knew this was the spot for it.

ABOVE: If you're not furnishing your stair landings, you're missing out. They're great for overflow party space, for reading a book, or just for giving yourself a place to rest on your way to the next floor. Stairs can be exhausting. **OPPOSITE:** Surprise! At the touch of a button, a flat-screen TV rises on hydraulics out of the console table at the foot of the bed in this guest room. (Believe it or not, back in the main bedroom, a screen also rises out of the back of the sofa.) I like putting curtains in front of window seats in bedrooms so you don't have to climb up on the cushions to close a bunch of shades at night.

ABOVE AND OPPOSITE: As long as I live, I don't think I will ever get to do another kiddo bedroom quite like this one, though I hope I do. A plaster-embellished ceiling and scenic botanical wallpaper plus embroidered curtains and a custom faux bois four-poster bed? I mean, come on! We added the ceiling adornment after picking the paper because we wanted it to look like some of the wall's vines had climbed overhead.

The owners' young son loved blue, which is one of my favorite colors to design with. But in a bedroom, it can look a little cold. I warmed things up with light honey-hued millwork and the soft textures of a grass cloth wall covering, a fuzzy rug, and woven textiles for the bed and bedding, plus the painting of three firetruck-red balls by John Gibson. The space is fun for a little kid and, I hope, mature enough to last him into his teenage years.

OPPOSITE AND FOLLOWING PAGES: If there's a single room that's the ultimate pièce de résistance within this house, it's this art deco–accented games room, lounge, and bar. Everything in here is custom, from the colors in the patchwork curtains, to the marbles used for the Ping-Pong table, to the pattern of the parquet floor, to the hair-on-hide rug. This is the spot for adults to gather—it's where I'd want to be—and it's always where the fun happens. As a result, this room needed to be more colorful and less serious than anywhere else in the house.

LIFE LESSON

Captain's Hour, Ahoy

A dozen years—and three houses—ago, a bit after our sons were born, my wife and I started an evening tradition we call "Captain's Hour." This was, and is, our sacred adults-only Us Time after the kids are in bed or, now that they're older, while they're playing by themselves or, I'll admit it, absorbed by their screens. It gives us a chance to connect and catch up and enjoy each other's company. (Or at least I enjoy Katie's company. You'll have to talk to her about whether she still enjoys mine. But what's not to love, right?) When we have friends over for dinner or staying the night, the hour expands to welcome any and all grown-ups in the house. Sometimes, there are cocktails involved. OK, often. OK, usually. But it's more about time away and apart from the younger ones, and about how that time apart makes us enjoy the time together even more. We now have a dedicated spot in our house for Captain's Hour. And I encourage everyone I work with to carve out a similar space. When you're trying to create time apart, it's helpful to have space apart, too. This Palm Beach house has an absolute dream of a grown-up getaway: an Italian art deco–inspired lounge-meets-games-room that's almost in a wing of its own. Best of all? It sports an absolutely epic bar hand-carved from a monumental thirteen-ton block of Breccia Capraia marble from Pietrasanta, Italy.

UNGALOW
G ON WATER

Texture and Good Taste

A YOUNG FAMILY OF FOUR GETS A SUMMER DREAM HOME WHERE OCEAN VIEWS PLAY A STARRING ROLE

If I ever design a house on the ocean for myself, I'd like it to look a lot like this one. Sure, I love a big-patterned, bold-contrast, blue-and-white beach house as much as anyone, maybe even more than anyone. (Wanna challenge me? Let's go!) But this highly textured, largely neutrally hued summer vacation home—which sits on a bit of the coast of New Jersey that's way more Hamptons than it is *Jersey Shore*—just feels so good to be in, I wouldn't want mine any other way.

A big part of that goodness, and the reason for keeping things neutral here, comes from the major water views: ocean on one side and bay on the other. I guess I could have tried to compete with that, but man, why bother? Instead, we went with something that would complement what was going on outside while keeping the focus squarely on those vistas.

OPPOSITE AND PREVIOUS PAGES: Throughout this coastal New Jersey home, and especially in the combined dining and living room, I used blue as if it was a neutral. Because it's what you see in the sea and sky out the windows, that only seemed natural. The color almost fades into the background, in a good way, like tan and taupe would elsewhere. **PAGE 218:** I mixed rough and smooth textures in the foyer.

I wanted to always be aware that the view was amazing, and I wanted anyone else in the house to always be aware of that, too. At the same time, I wanted to design each room to be just interesting enough that you'd want to look at and enjoy the interiors as well.

OK, but what does all that mean? In this house—a shingle-style new build with an old soul—it meant using some key pieces of mid-century furniture to create a very collected-looking interior that flows well from one room to the next, with nothing too fussy or formal. Hits of texture and character come from the grass cloth covering a lot of the walls, from the wicker lamp shades and rope-covered beds used here and there, and from interesting vintage pieces like the lights and chairs in the great room. And neutral in this house didn't just mean beige and greige and ivory and taupe and ecru and tan and all their other friends and relations. When designing by the water, I think blue can also be a neutral, and, here, I definitely used it that way.

The husband-and-wife owners have two young kids, as well as great, sophisticated taste and a major love of mid-century modern furniture and contemporary art. I did their main home in Florida (page 191) just before this, which got a majorly neutral look. But where that one is also majorly luxe—while still being family-friendly—they wanted this one to be more relaxed, and even family-friendlier. Some of that relaxation comes from

LIFE LESSON

Kitchen Confidential

Kitchens, man—they're expensive. And it always seems like there's a domino effect with them, as there can be with so many construction projects. You start by wanting to make one little cosmetic change, and the next thing you know, you're halfway to a gut renovation. When the family I worked with here bought this house, the place had just been built, and even though they didn't love everything about its kitchen, they really didn't love the idea of completely reconstructing a complex room whose paint had barely had time to dry. So, instead of going back to the drawing board, and sending ourselves down a redesign rabbit hole, we just made some big-impact, low-stress changes: new farmhouse-chic pendants over the island to provide a pop of color, and a new diamond-shaped tile backsplash to provide unexpected graphic pattern and texture. These notes help distract from some of the slightly discordant, less-than-ideal architectural features. And they didn't break the bank, either.

OPPOSITE: When you've got a kitchen like this one, that's entirely open to the formal dining and living areas, you want it to look like it's of a piece with those entertaining spaces, but also like it's not trying to steal the spotlight. This new-build house came with a white-on-white kitchen that was already pretty quiet. We just added a couple of different accent elements so it would feel as finished as the decorating elsewhere.

using overstuffed upholstered pieces and, of course, indoor-outdoor and other hard-to-destroy materials pretty much everywhere.

A lot of it also comes from being a bit heavier in the use of real color, especially blue hues and most of all in smaller rooms with less-sensational views. Even though there's color here, I didn't mix several hues together in any one space. Instead, I used big swaths of the same or very similar ones. When I did combine two colors, it was usually two that are closely related, like the dark blue and dark green of the double bedroom. They're so similar, they almost read as one color.

A big thing that keeps this neutral place exciting, even with all its neutrality, is the interesting contemporary light fixtures. The owners realized that if we changed out the existing, nondescript pendants and chandeliers, the whole place would feel much more custom. And you know what? Dude was right!

Last major note about this place is its outdoor space. The summer weather here is near-perfect, so I wanted this family's porches, decks, and patios to feel just as warm and inviting as the rest of the house. The best way to do that? Help these outdoor rooms be true extensions of the interior spaces they open from, continuing the colors, textures, and materials from one to the next. That's just what I did, and now this family basically lives outside as much as they possibly can, and in as much relaxed comfort and style as they do in their living, dining, and bedrooms.

OPPOSITE: If you've got room for them in your main suite, I always like to put a pair of armchairs at the foot of a bed rather than a bench. That way, a couple can use them to sit down and actually talk to each other, while a bench is more just for putting on shoes and packing suitcases. **PREVIOUS PAGES:** The TV room takes a slight break from all the blue hues.

ABOVE: A subtle, soothing gray palette gives this bathroom a spa-like vibe. The window placement wasn't great, but we made the most of it with this quirky oval-shaped, rattan-framed mirror. **OPPOSITE:** The patterned curtains and wall covering work perfectly together in this guest room because their prints are of two such different scales—one pretty small and fairly soft, the other way more graphic and bold—but their colors are almost identical. Something about it just calls my name for a nap.

ABOVE AND OPPOSITE: This house's architect originally conceived this space as a closet. It's way more fun now, right? The kids who constantly jump from bed to bed certainly think so. The cabinetry by the window stores all their toys. **FOLLOWING PAGES:** Since this place is all about its water and sky views and its beach and ocean access, the outdoor spaces had to be as finished as the interior—and boy, are they. In fact, I developed the color and material palette for the porches first, then brought them inside.

Modernism Made Warm

SHOWING OFF THE SOFTER SIDE OF INDUSTRIAL—WITH A TRADITIONAL TWIST—FOR A FAMILY OF SIX IN TEXAS

I'm kicking this one off with a sports metaphor, so bear with me. Ready? Here goes: When it comes to interiors, a modern house is kind of like a football team that doesn't need a single superstar. Instead, every player needs to do their job, they need to be good at it, and they need to work together to complement each other equally well. Traditional style is more often like the team with a single mega star who everyone else supports. At least, that's how it works in my admittedly sort-of-twisted head.

So, in a classically minded house, I usually start off a room, or even the whole place, with one really special patterned rug or textile, or a spectacular piece of art, that serves as the lead for the entire project. In a modern one, I instead try to think more about everything everywhere all at once.

When I'm designing with neutral tones, I like leaning into art and rugs that provide some interesting texture. These pieces can make a statement similar to what color does in a more brightly hued space. That idea worked perfectly in the modernist marvel that is this new-build home in Austin, Texas—especially in the serene living room. **PREVIOUS PAGES:** Sitting under the foyer's gravity-defying staircase is a console made from an old elm tree on the property.

HOTEL SPACES
Michael Howard
ATMOSPHERE

The house's hilltop setting offers amazing vistas of Downtown Austin. The scene from this sitting room is great during the day, but even better at night when the skyline lights up. I used curtains to frame and draw attention to the view.

Ron Galella

For the dining area, I knew I wanted to find a piece of art for the back wall that looked like it was coming out into the room as if it was a sculpture. At the same time, I knew we needed something with tones that would blend with the rest of the design and not compete with the views. This piece just nailed it. As for the custom oak table, it's wide enough to fit two at either end when needed. The more the merrier!

LIFE LESSON

The Materials Are the Message

To get this place to look its best—and best accommodate the family that would call it home—I knew I wanted to link the house's modernist-glass-box architecture with the owners' desire for some traditional furniture and plenty of creature comforts. That meant making the most of natural materials that could warm up the cool contemporary design and largely neutral color palette. The house's velvety Venetian plaster walls in a pale ecru help the whole place feel warm and inviting. To soften any remaining hard edges, I added texture-rich woven fabrics and hand-knotted rugs. I also used plenty of deeply hued, richly grained wood to enhance a sense of warmth.

The study does double duty as a guest bedroom thanks to a Murphy bed that ingeniously pops out of a wall. I designed the tall cabinets to be multipurpose, able to hold office supplies, overnight guests' clothes, and more. **PREVIOUS PAGES:** This family of six loves to have movie nights, so a big, cozy, sectional sofa was a requirement for their family room. Because the view from this space isn't great, we could make the TV the focal point.

That was certainly the case here, in an awesome new-build house, in Austin, Texas, whose distinctive architecture—all sleek lines, right angles, huge expanses of glass, high ceilings, blackened steel, polished wood, and Venetian plaster walls—gave it a distinctly modern point of view. That's something I love, and, if I'm being honest, I don't do enough of it, though modern is probably my favorite style. It gets me mega-energized.

This place was especially interesting because the owners, a couple with four school-age kids, also had a traditional bent. I think this home is my studio's best version yet of creating a slightly traditional-leaning interior that works great in a modern house. The combination blends so well here because the palette complements the architecture even though the styles of the interior and the exterior are a bit different.

In fact, the architecture, both inside and out, is what led to the neutral palette. The slight sheen and natural tone of the plaster just called out for a subtle touch. And we went with what it was saying. The plan didn't need to be overthought: I knew I needed to (a) respect the sparkling city views from the stellar hilltop location, (b) make the furnishings comfy and durable for this fun-loving family, and (c) pick light, neutrally hued fabrics that enhance the amazing plaster walls.

With this plan in mind, the design all came together very quickly. On an early trip

I chose a very dark hue for the four-poster bed in the main suite to echo the blackened-steel window frames. I then lightened things up by using soothing blues for other elements of the space.

after I first saw the house, I flew back to Austin with a very large bag of neutral, nicely textured fabrics. We sat in the living room, which was empty, and laid everything out on the floor and designed the entire house in one day. And it was a huge success. We looked at all our players together, all at once, so they'd each do their job for the team, and they did. Things changed here and there, of course, but we did the overall look and flow of the house in that room that day. I wish everything was so easy.

For me, what ultimately makes this house a winner is that it's all about great shapes. We custom-made almost all the wood pieces you see here, and their forms are just so intriguing to look at as you move from room to room. That keeps the neutral scheme from getting monotonous. Take a peek at the entryway, where the zigzag pattern of the console table base—made from an old elm tree that had to be removed from the property—grabs your attention. Or, check out the broad, layered legs on the white oak kitchen table and the sexy curves on some of the cane armchairs.

Since finishing this place, I've been lucky enough to return for get-togethers, and let me tell you, it's a house that everyone wants to be in, and the parties are always fantastic. As a designer, when you get to see the people you worked with enjoying their home, and you get to be a part of that, it truly is the most rewarding thing.

The house's ample square footage meant the homeowners had room in their bedroom for a relaxing sitting area—a great luxury if you can fit it in. This tranquil nook has proved itself as fun and fantastic in the morning for coffee as at night with a glass of wine. I love how the artwork suggests that daytime/nighttime thing.

This covered porch serves a ton of great purposes. As you can see, it's broad enough for a very large seating and lounging area, plus one for dining, and an outdoor kitchen beyond. The large roof here also helps shade the house from the hot Texas sun. Mindful that the overhang might make the interior rooms feel dark, we added square skylights for a little extra brightness. The pool house beyond, which holds the home's joint office and guest room space, has glass walls that let it all but disappear as it gets to the edge of the property.

Acknowledgments

I'm never at a loss for words, so I'm not gonna lie to you and say that I am—even though my overwhelming gratitude for all the people who helped create these houses and this book leaves me pretty speechless.

First, to all the owners who let me into your lives to help you create the houses you now call home, thank you. None of this would be possible without you, and that's no exaggeration. The same is true about the team of designers who I'm lucky enough to work with every day: Kelsey Heneveld, Meg Hickey, and Lindsey Waters. You all make me look good, which is no easy task sometimes (just ask my wife and kids).

Our designs get to fill the rooms of some amazing houses. So to architects Daniel Kahan, Kevin Gray, Cronk Duch, Stan Dixon, and Portuondo Perotti, I salute you, and all I've learned from you. The construction and build teams we architects and designers collaborate with have the task of taking what sometimes seems impossible and making it beautifully possible. The hoops I've asked pros including RWB Construction, Cottage Home Company, Scott Simpson, and Jomed Construction to jump through have been pretty high, but they've never missed. I can say the same about the artisans we work with—cabinetmaker River City, upholsterer Aaron Richmond, decorative painters Bob Christian, Stephen Floyd, Gracie Studio, and so many more—all of whom have become adopted members of our in-house team.

The photographers and stylists who come together to show these houses in their absolute best light are another huge part of what makes this book a success. Photographers Eric Piasecki (who shot eight of the houses here), plus Noe Dewitt, David Land, and Lucas Allen; and stylists Helen Crowther (who handled eleven homes) and Chelsea Donnan: What you do is a mystery to me, but please keep doing it. I owe you big time.

This book really owes its existence to Shawna Mullen at Abrams, who, for some reason, trusted me enough after book one to let me do a second. Her capable crew—Danny Maloney, Krista Keplinger, and Katie Gaffney—is the reason you're holding this book in your hands right now. Helping me get it to Abrams were go-to book designer Doug Turshen and his next in command, David Huang, plus writer, editor, friend, and the guy I call "my brother from another mother," Andrew Sessa. They hit it out of the park again.

Finally, I've got to bring it back to family. If you've made it this far into this book, you've realized by now that it's the families who own and go on to live in these houses that are the heart of each of these homes. That's true in my life as well. To my parents, my wife, and my kids, thank you, thank you, thank you, thank you, thank you, thank you times a million. For encouraging me, for listening to me, for lifting me up when I'm down, and for bringing me back to earth when I'm flying too close to the sun. (Who, me? Nah. Never.) Most of all, though, thank you for making me laugh more than any other group of people in the world.

Oh yeah, and hey! You! Yes, you! Thank you, dear reader, for holding this book in your hand. You rock, too.

About the Author

A true passion for helping families create the places they call home is in Andrew Howard's DNA. As the son of celebrated interiors masters James Michael Howard and Phoebe Howard, Andrew got his start in the design business working in one of his parents' Jacksonville, Florida, home stores. Those early days in the shop saw him handling the heavy lifting—literally. On his first morning on the job, he managed to lug in a marble mantel using a barely functioning dolly.

Fast forward twenty years, and Andrew has established himself as a go-to designer for young families setting up house, whether in cities big or small or coveted countryside destinations. Celebrated for his unique ability to combine color and pattern in engagingly playful but still sophisticated ways, he has an innate understanding of what makes a house work for kids. Hint: Stain proofing everything and using outdoor fabrics everywhere—lessons Andrew and his wife, Katie, have learned well as parents to their two boys.

Writer and editor Andrew Sessa is a regular contributor to *Architectural Digest*, *Travel & Leisure*, and many other design and travel publications. He co-authored *Style Comfort Home* (Abrams, 2021) with Andrew Howard and recently created *The Waterfront House* (Abrams, 2025) with Phoebe Howard. This is his ninth book.

Editor: Shawna Mullen
Designer: Doug Turshen with David Huang
Design Manager: Danny Maloney
Managing Editor: Krista Keplinger
Production Manager: Katie Gaffney

Library of Congress Control Number: 2024948414

ISBN: 978-1-4197-7465-2
eISBN: 979-8-88707-322-4

Printed and bound in China
10 9 8 7 6 5 4 3 2 1

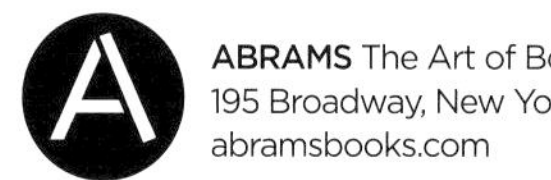